late
MOON

OTHER BOOKS
BY PAMELA PORTER

No Ordinary Place,
Ronsdale Press, 2012

I'll Be Watching,
Groundwood Books, 2011

This Awakening to Light,
Leaf Press, 2010

Cathedral, Ronsdale Press, 2010

The Intelligence of Animals,
The Backwaters Press, 2008

Yellow Moon, Apple Moon,
Groundwood Books, 2008

Stones Call Out, Coteau Books, 2006

The Crazy Man,
Groundwood Books, 2005

Sky, Groundwood Books, 2004

Poems for the Luminous World,
Frog Hollow Press, 2002

late MOON

PAMELA PORTER

RONSDALE

LATE MOON
Copyright © 2013 Pamela Porter

RONSDALE PRESS
3350 West 21st Avenue
Vancouver, B.C., Canada V6S 1G7
www.ronsdalepress.com

Typesetting: Julie Cochrane, in New Baskerville 11 pt on 13.5
Cover Design: Julie Cochrane
Paper: Ancient Forest Friendly Rolland Opaque — 100% post-consumer
     waste, totally chlorine-free and acid-free

Ronsdale Press wishes to thank the following for their support of its publishing program: the Canada Council for the Arts, the Government of Canada through the Canada Book Fund, the British Columbia Arts Council, and the Province of British Columbia through the Book Publishing Tax Credit Program.

Library and Archives Canada Cataloguing in Publication

Porter, Pamela, 1956–
    Late moon / Pamela Porter.

Poems.
ISBN 978-1-55380-236-5 (print)
ISBN 978-1-55380-237-2 (ebook) / ISBN 978-1-55380-238-9 (pdf)

    I. Title.

PS8581.O7573L38 2013   C811'.6   C2012-907710-0

At Ronsdale Press we are committed to protecting the environment. To this end we are working with Canopy (formerly Markets Initiative) and printers to phase out our use of paper produced from ancient forests. This book is one step towards that goal.

Printed in Canada by Marquis Book Printing, Quebec, Canada

for Rob,
Cecilia and Drew,
my dear ones,

and for my fathers

ACKNOWLEDGEMENTS

I would like to acknowledge those journals in which poems from this book first appeared: *Atlanta Review, CV2, Connotation Press, Descant, Prism International, The New Quarterly.*

"My Father in His Garden, Depicted in the Woodblock Print of the Taishō Dynasty" won the 2011 Prism International Prize. "The Place of Feathers" received honourable mention in the *Descant* Best Canadian Poem contest.

"And in What Darkness" was inspired by the line "What vanished and in what light," in Patrick Lane's uncollected poem "I'll Leave the Door Open a Little."

"Mercy" was inspired by Lorna Crozier's poem "A Good Day to Start a Journal," from *Everything Arrives at the Light.* "Apprentice" was inspired by "Indigo," from *The Garden Going On Without Us.*

The title of the poem "At Night for Long Hours I Hear Songs" was taken from the diary of Frédéric Chopin.

"The Night Has Six Moons" is for Rod.

"Winter" is for Nancy.

"The Place of Feathers" is for Rob.

I wish to express my gratitude to everyone at Ronsdale Press, especially Ron Hatch, for their continued support of my work. I would like to thank Russell Thorburn, who brought his exquisite sensitivities again to this manuscript, and who threaded the poems together as only he can do. I want to thank my fellow poets at Planet Earth Poetry, the Ocean Wilderness and Honeymoon Bay retreats, and the Waywords for their support and encouragement. Finally, I would like to thank Lorna Crozier and Patrick Lane; because of you I have come this far.

CONTENTS

ALL THIS TIME

—

Evening grows late, light slow,
*   echo of the day's bright bell*
calling and calling the fathers in.

Evening holds out a cup of light
in case her father arrives thirsty,
*   ripens the tree's fruit*
in case he is hungry.

I go to unlock room
*   after room of the night*
in case my father arrives weary.
*   One by one the sky*
sets the stars on fire,

and we wait for our fathers,
our lost fathers, whose daughters
remain watchful,
*   our torches lit.*

We will unfold blankets over them,
stroke their heads
*   silver as moonlight,*
rejoicing, should they arrive,

our fathers, who all this time
did not know
*   their need of us.*

– I –

My Questions Go Unanswered

Tonight my father, as a young man, is wandering
the darkness above my head, lost
in the thin hills west of Hermosillo.
　　　　　And the child I once was
paces room after room, looking for him.

Some nights I don't sleep for the two of them.
　　　　　One lost, one searching.

Beneath his boots, sand scours stone,
his ear to the elf owls,
　　　　　　　small as sparrows
in the pale flowers of the Saguaro.

　　　　In her nightgown, she sweeps
past halls and doorways, skims
　　　the staircase.
　　　　　　　I want to tell her
it's her fatherlessness keeps me awake;
it's his wandering alone makes me want
　　　　　　　to rescue him.

There's a thin blade of moon out,
and she won't rest until she finds him.
A scholar of pain, he has too many
　　　　　years of study left to him.

Now I hear her climbing to the roof.
She's trying to see over the curve of earth,
catch the song of the smallest owl
　　　　　　　in the world.

Where is God tonight, the one
who made love so difficult, our lives
            filled with estrangement?
This night as every night, my questions
go unanswered, even as I know
            their futures, as I know
by her standing on the roof, she's thinking
if she believes purely enough,
            she could open her arms and fly.

Hungering

Full morning, the men in the field
standing in the bed of the truck,
      heaving bales of hay
with a steady drumbeat onto the floor
of the barn, and high in the trees, the owls
      are calling again.
I have heard them in the night,
a sound like a wooden flute, and know
each is hungering for the other
hidden
      in the congregation of pines.
The male, earnest, fervent, an element
of concern in his notes, waits
      until its mate answers,
and then the frantic rustle of wings
toward a closer pine.
      Orbital, planetary,
just shy of panic
      is their longing for the other,
made to be, like us, spun blind by love
that feels as much
      like sickness unto death,
the beloved the only cure.
      For years
my father kept an owl in the freezer,
bound by his need for it,
      the glassed eyes,
the beak's slow curve, the frozen wings
      part of his own lost wildness,
as though a part of his soul
had stretched its mottled wings
      and flown into the night.

I, too, have chained myself
           as one indentured to mystery,
the stars' high singing and the moon
flying over the trees,

when that loneliness overtakes me
and I'm famished,
tethered to my loves soul to soul,
         my palms pressed
to the drumbeat in their chests,
that which holds the spirit down.
Now the truck clatters down the lane,
loosed specks of hay dust floating in air,
        pieces of light
               broken off the sun.
And the owls, high in the high pines.

A sudden rush of wings and gone —
not even the sweetest birdsong
          could assuage such grief.

Poetry

One day, Poetry entered me.
I don't know precisely
                where or when.
I was young. A child.
While my parents argued
                in a darkening room,
                I stood behind them.
I heard them speak my name.
I learned what my mother had done.

It was around this time
                Poetry entered me,
a bird of purled smoke
as if from a smothered fire, a bird
who folded her wings and hid
inside my darkness.

I saw that my father had gone,
and that others had lost their faces.
The night left me alone
to wander its endless rooms.

As I grew I began to hear
                the leaf's litany of grief
whispered to the branch,
ground beetles' secrets spilled
                to the rain
and the bitter grasses' to the frost.
Poetry sat up in me
                and sang her evensong,
promising we could tell the truth,
                she and I,
promising we could tell everything.

The River Asked Me

When the river asked me
where was the path
            to my father's house
while begging the stone coins
of his own father,
I didn't know which I'd find —
the father watching at the window
or the one in hiding
            behind the mountain.

I didn't know then all the ways
leaving resembles arriving,
couldn't tell the colour of the moon
            setting into the sea
from my own *amen*.

And what did she see, Moon,
            before she drowned,
but my father lying down to die
just before I raised my knocking fist
            to his door?
            In truth,
he was a withered blossom
            ripening into fruit,
a man between two countries —
            ruin and beginning —
a man who would awaken
            a stranger to himself
            while I visited his dreams
as beggar, thief,
            wraith on the darkened stairs,
my mouth filled with stars
and the road's dust.

Perhaps it's why neither of us
can stop remembering,

his voice the dawn to a morning
in which the frost burns away each hour,
his dreams
        the dawn to an evening

in which the moon starts over, .
thin from her own dying,
            and buys her passage
with the fragrance of jasmine
mixed with the future's tears.

In Both My Hands

My father who wanted to die
      is now content with living.
And my father who wanted to go on living,
    now is content with death.

I balance them in both my hands
      whose lamps I orbit,
            little planet,
     winter's moth.

One unwrapped his losses and lived.
    One folded up his joys and died,
both alive in me
     along with the wild animal
        who is God.

The blind stars give and give away their light
while the moon remains
          deaf to its own silence,
and on their backs the weightless birds
     carry the sky —

this, the mystery by which all things
are connected —
what enters, unstoppable,
    and makes its refuge,
      the small sabbath
that does not care if we are faithless,
my fathers, living and dead,
    and God's paw print
in the snow at morning,
    his breath still frozen on the air.

Land's End

The waves were not bells
though they tolled over and over,
the news written in the cliffs —
                    shells long buried,
formed into script, ornate, elegant —
that it was ordained,
that it fell to him
                    to be my father,
the post abandoned by more
than could be counted — a line of men
like a host of heaven
who scraped my childhood
                    with their leaving.

We made our way over driftwood, beneath
the trees' exposed roots, leaves
                    pared by wind,
the waves tolling again and again
while the sun, pale bear, foraged
                    down the slope of the sky.

And what I carried through my life,
the stone weight of it
                    that would have drowned me
had I walked into the sea with it,
was what no man wanted from me —
                    devotion spared of lust,
untarnished, child-like,
                    an embarrassment of riches,

a vineyard. It fell to him
to receive it, bushel upon bushel,
all my stores of love tangled up with lust
claimed, vied for, but this —
recorded in the verses spelled out
                            by the shells
that I should not go down to dust
before I gave it away,
pristine, pure as the winter air.
                    It fell to him,
so said the ancient bone, so said the tide,
the foam, the blown trees laid down,
the myriad stones,
            his thinned and silvered hair
glinting as the conflagrations of birds
bright on the waters.

I spread my fingers over the wall
where it was written ages ago
before I ever dreamed my breath.
He studied the script. I traced its Braille.

The Night Has Six Moons

Here are the letters you never received,
bundled in ancient string.
Envelopes stamped
            by rain and tears.
Addresses worn down
to wisps of smoke
            that burn the eyes.

They say, *Morning arrived*
                on schedule again today.
Birdsong and new leaves.

They say, *Sun wandered all day across the sky*
                with its hands in its pockets.

They tell of the heartbreaking
            beauty of the world,
and how, without one's glasses,
the night has six moons, all cousins,
                how a leaf of the winter past
lies folded on the pasture fence,
      a letter from the sky
                    to the field
full yellow now with blossoms,

a parchment covered with small dark
                cracks of script:
      All the bitter winter
I have waited for you, sleeping so
beneath the snow.
      Across days and nights,
                across dreams and calling,
      I am waiting
please, am waiting for you.

Elk at Evening with Horses Grazing

He does not pretend
        to be one of them,
standing alert in the field among
the grazing horses. How he arrived

inside the fenced periphery of grasses
I do not know. How did Christ
        roll away the stone?
But the horses are not troubled
by his presence,
        growing as he is
out of the dark roots of his hooves
with the stillness of a tree.

In his branches lie tangled all manner
        of thing — moss, fern,
my living father's earth-stained glove,
my dead father's necktie,
        my mother's letters, perfumed.

        Last night as I slept,
he ranged through the undergrowth
of my life, while birds perched
on the tips of his lovely horns,
        straw in their beaks, fur,
        the high, cold moon
caught in the antlers of the trees.

Standing in the Sky

The photograph was lost, somewhere
between intention and *yes,*
      between moonrise and refrain.
I will not find it again
though I search all the uncounted
      rooms of my life.

A bright day, the winter shore.
The great boulders lay
      in their great sleep.
He scaled a rocky height, called for me,
and I climbed, balancing on the fallen
trees, the accumulated years
      of searching for him,
of candles lit and drowned in their wells.

We were laughing, standing in the sky
      like a memory of heaven,
while the sea sang its drinking songs,
and birds opened and closed the bright petals
      of their wings.
I leaned into his gentleness then,
      tucked under his arm;
below us, a lens opened and shut,
some ghostly part of us caught inside it.

Those who have died and come back
say, *I understood everything,*
      everything —
what slips away while we sleep,
what the sea prays for under its breath.

The photograph was icon,
            to place my finger on, to say,

            Before my birth I knew you,
and put on grief to find you,
            a shawl of broken moon —
A day or a life is mortal as a leaf
            flung from the tree,
as dusk's furnace setting the pines alight.
We stood on a rock,
            stood in the air,
triumphant, the moment flying,
            the winter-blown sky.

Little Father

When I look into the yellow rose, Father,
      I find you sleeping there.
Is it that you wish to be lonely,
or that you never wanted a daughter,
      or does the sullen autumn sun
keep you dreaming and cold?

Father whose forehead I stroke
with my finger tip,
      I would give you wings
so when I find you nosing at my window,
      I would cup you in my hand
and bring you in.
      My father, my moth,
I would exchange your tears for my tears.
      I would lie down
and be your road out of darkness.

Under the autumn sun I lay you down
      to sleep in my heart,
a room whose curtainless windows
let your dreams fly in and out,
whose doors
      allow a stranger music.

Wine of my blood given for you,
heart that beats within my heart,
      little father
who sleeps on and on in me.

− II −

Just My Life

Tonight my dead father is tapping at my window.
How lonely he seems, there in the dark,
wind whipping his robe, unravelling his hair.
                    It's cold outside.
Someone should let him in.

                    I want to tell my father
he doesn't need to arrive unnoticed.
        My mother is no longer waiting for him.
The neighbours aren't watching.

If he is longing for books, he can read mine.
If he is hungry for darkness,
                I have enough to share.
I want to tell him there is no need for sadness.
The rain takes care of that.

When he taps at the window,
        let him rush in on the wind,
let the candle's flame bow before him. After all,
what he believed was a mistake
                    was just my life.
My mother opened the door.
He entered, I slithered between them,
        and we met,
my father emptying his pockets
                    of dust and coins
which I carried into the world
in both my fists, the taste of him
                secreted on my tongue.

The Letter

You walk from room to room
reading a book
           of Chinese poetry.
Outside, flowers wave to the wind
as the sea waves to its lover,
           the moon.

Your walking, your holding
the book of ancient verse,
is like a woman
           holding a letter,
who slips the paper
from the envelope,
           stamped,
cancelled, addressed
to her, this house, that road
           skimming the sea
and covered a little with sand.
She, too, walks slowly,

deliberately
from room to room. Outside,
           the white blossoms
of the apple tree. But the letter
tells her she is not the woman
she thought herself to be.

It is spring, and it is winter.
In her letter, blossoms are folding
           back into buds.
Her father is not her father,
her mother holding the secret
for so long.

In the book of Chinese poetry,
candles light other candles;
crows leave the sky
            one by one.

The woman checks the envelope,
addressed only to her.

She had hoped, somehow,
to find the name wrong,
            the handwriting
unrecognizable. But her name,
in script on the envelope,
            unmistakable,
is like the axe-blow in the poem
of the Chinese poet, a sharp
            scent of pine, blossoms
scattering in air, turning
            to snow,

and suddenly the seasons reverse.
For the woman,
            it is winter
while you are walking into spring,
a certain joy in your loneliness,

the mad girl in the poem
laughing,
            the river's currents
careening her boat toward night.

Baptism

I want to be the one to assist now,
write my name as witness.
        I'm old enough,
fugitive from my own life.
Like you, I'd put on robes, open
the book to the page. I'd recite, for once,
the words I was told to.
             No making things up.

It would be a bright morning
just like the day you came to the house —
so much time I'd spent trimming lamps!
        Oh, yes,
            for my magdalene mother
and the bridegroom come at last.

When I'm brought down the aisle
in receiving blankets,
        the windows' light bruising us
through stained-glass, the one
where Judas is paid his shekels of silver,
I'd be the one to watch
        for a silent exchange
from my mother's eyes to yours,
while the man who stands beside her
quietly buries his disbelief.

And when you take me into your arms
and press holy water on my head,
I'd lean close
        to my infant self, place
my ear to your heart and listen
for anything I could call love.

Or not. I can handle the truth.
Truth is,
      I left the ship's hold of your hands
and returned to my life —
the moneychangers, the enduring dust —

and learned to put my treasure
in weeds flowering among the ruins,
the taste of stone on my tongue,
      in the rooms inside myself
where you reside
with your theology, your angelic choirs,
            midnight stars —
what remains for me
      to squander or to inherit.

The Shape of My Father's Face

is the stone
that trips me in the dark. It is the night
of an oblong moon
and the storm that erases the moon.

My father's face is in the air
between sorrow and remembrance,
between the frayed hem of dream
and the dream unravelled.
It is the shape of water
escaping the cup of my hands,
it is moonlight
searching the depths of the pond.

The shape of my father's face
travels the length of loss,
the height and breadth
of absence.
It floats on the clear bell of silence.

It is the weight of a locked door,
the lightness of the hand
without a key,
the swiftness of a bird
rising beyond sight.

To Speak of Him

To speak of him, I might say, *absent,*
meaning *winter,* a long darkness.
                    As in *an absence of stars.*
I might say, *echo,*
            a father who dwelt at the bottom
of an abyss, a canyon.

To speak of him I might use *silent,*
the light of afternoon leaving a doorway,
                    the shadow of a barn
lengthening over a field;
            a road no one travels.

I could say, *deserted,* as though
he went to live in a desert,
            a mountain range risen up
between us, the nights a moon
                    frozen to the sky.
Or perhaps, *vanished,* meaning
the shape he left in air,
            or *God's magician,*
another father put in his place, an actor, imposter.

I could say he was *unreachable,* a face
lonely behind a glass,
                    a window.
For *lonely,* I put rain on the glass.
I set absence there, I place silence
                    and an echo, vanishing.
Unreachable, he grew old, his arms
                    branches without leaves.

And like the sound of geese
beating their wings and crying to the night,
    all these have entered me:
        canyon, shadow, mountain,
a long season,
        the frozen moon, and the rain.

Rune

I bury my mother in the dawn.
Now she rises in me each morning,
my table set, the spoon
I lift to her mouth
                a moon of milk,
and all the clocks run backward
into rose, and fence, and thorn.

I bury my mother in my mind.
Now the blood maples set sail
                over the hurried carts
of the dead, a wind
                blowing out the candles.
I place her hands together,
                fold them on her lap
and pay the jailer to hand me
                the iron ring, the keys.

I bury my mother in the night.
Now she comes to my bed
                in her ghost dress
and names me *bastard of God,*
                shame's darling.
I become a fox crossing the snow,
I hold her in my mouth,
                a wafer on my tongue.

I bury my mother alive
so I might live with her in the grave.
Now I sweep its many rooms.
I open the book of hours
                 and read to her,
hour after hour, page by page,
my finger slow beneath each word.
Forgive, it says.
Every word, *forgive.*

Why I Came Down

Because the morning arrived
                    bloodied,
though no more so than any other.
Because others returned
telling of wondrous things.
          Because of the dog,

and striations of mountain
          in the long light of dawn,
and the hushed, unnameable
          whiteness of snow. Because
I had heard of the embroidery of spider
in the air between barn and window.

Because I was eager to see my loneliness
                    ripen into grief. Because
my hair would give my father away, and he
would go away then, without me,
          though the world would persist
                    in its astonishments.

Because I was allowed to carry
          the dimmed lint of heaven
in my fists. Because a drop of shame
burned silently in each of us.
Because I could almost feel my father's hands
on the hospital glass.

Because this is what I was given,
          and because love quickens, even
in the slightest fissure
                    of a stone.

After Rain

Meadow glazed with sun,
three horses with thickening fur
                graze the field,
their backs and the grasses steaming
like the white plumes
           of their breath
now, at night beneath the moon.

Apples ripened, falling, one by one.
             The long shadows of pines
shake summer from their manes.

Apprentice

I will go now
to your vacant house
beneath the mountain
of scrub and pine.

I your shadow,
your secret, your
little cactus.
I will go now

to your vacant house
and I will walk around
in the great caverns
of your shoes. At last

I will put my arms inside
the arms of your shirts
and I will wear one over
the other over the other.

I will run my fingers along
the pleats in your trousers,
regard the icons of your belts
and your ties.

I will open cupboards and drawers
and behold your cereal bowl,
your grapefruit spoons.
So much to learn.

Every day of my life your absence grew
in my eyes, my breath.
Unlike like your legitimate children
with their airy forgetfulness,

I must memorize every detail, study
how the sun settled each evening
in the accumulated days and years
until your death.

Many more years of practice
will I require
in the profundity of your silence
before I may earn your name.

Seeker of Lost Souls

They lifted their lanterns around me,
one stroking my hair. I would forget
      everything, they said.
It's only human.
      But I vowed in secret
            to remember,
rehearsed over and over
the lamps of veil, the woven skeps,
the vast, uncountable portals,
              the cairns.
And set off then, my arms aching
carrying my soul
         in folds of fabric
pressed in the spines of a book,
that long distance in the dark.
The cactus, the detritus.

      In those first years
came dreams of snow filling
the crevassed, the plowed fields,
black birds
      calling and crying,
the scrap of names, addresses I'd lost
in the nether lands, stolen perhaps,
by those whose faces
      and hands were marked
by the terrible wanting.

I knew not to return until I'd found
      them all, list or no,
bewildered in their lives.
      The potholed, frozen roads,
burrs in my socks, the great,

                        grained steppes
I crossed, fires of dusk burning my eyes,
            and still did not forget,
my grief a blown glass, a window,
            the other side seen through,
misshapen but real nevertheless.

Who makes the rules, who decides
if we are launched, explorers, discoverers
                        through drought, monsoon,
all manner of weather,
our boats leaking, our mud huts
                        in ruin?
In time, it began —
            first the small details —
shades of colour, scents, the music
heard in stillness, then
I began to lose the larger things —
faces of those who saw me off
            and pressed their hands on mine.

And like one presumed lost
and for whom the search is called off,
I began to record, methodical, detailed,
what would remind me, feed me,
marked by date and time:

how the light fell, 5 p.m.
                        Luminous — my note.
January 5th — blade of grass in snow.
Tues. — bucket of rainwater, rent wings.
Morning, early — fantastic — ghost ships of cloud.

Last night, had a dream of orchards —
            no place I have seen on earth.

Wild Horse

He is standing in the rain
in the field at summer's end, the land
gone brown, the rain driving down
what remains of the grass, his mane
the colour of the grass, his back
          stained with rain,

though he stands beneath a lone pine,
looking into the granulated air.
        He must learn now,
must allow their hands on him,
the touch between his eyes,
     the stroke down his neck.

Within these lines of fence
lie all the wild there is for him — the land
        tamed, leaves flamed
and floating on the air, even
the rain.
       This is all there is now,
all the wild there is.

Late Moon

You went home then to your wife,
your daughter and son,
                    the moon
just begun to be born for the night,
and I, the thin smoke of candle,
the steam
          of your breath in the dark,
I the leaf floating down.

I was the one who made my mother's
                    hands burn,
and I who would steal the flame
of your hair.
          You drove home as the moon
lit the pale faces of your children,
                    as my mother
folded herself and slept
among the crumpled sheets,
          the silence saying its prayers,
the moon rising like the swollen
          belly of a woman.

From this moment on, you will lie
outside the light
          of your own forgiveness.
You know this before you slide into bed
under your roof
          beneath the milky way, the moon
a thin sacrament on your tongue.

And I, your little budding rose,
your stem of thorns, grow lovely
in dreams you will learn to forget,

        though the moon
chants its ancient hymn, its secret text
unfurled across the bed.

You read its verses all night.

– III –

When You Let Me Go

I remember the day, the gentle
shove from your hands,
                    the quiet water.
The current took over then,
my basket nudged downstream.

I waved my infant fists around
in the humid air. Crickets
                    played lullabies,
reeds folded themselves over me
and stroked my forehead like a father.

There were snakes, yes,
but I held my eyes shut.
I did not want to see the blue
                    floating world,
your footfalls on the hard shore leaving,
                    drumming my ears.

I sailed on in this manner,
                    my steady growing
as manna fell from clouds.
By the time my basket ran aground,
        I had grown enough,

                    tried the earth
and stood on my two feet. Thus,
I raised myself,
                    and sometimes wished
        I had drowned.

All Things Which Pass

Mother believed
    the secret would keep.
What she didn't plan on
        was the way
the body remembers, how
the man who fathered me
        rides along my veins
like the morning he drove away
down our autumn street,
    off to deal out forgiveness
to his parish, kneel at the altar
        of silence.

        I watched him go,
the distant mountains watching, too,
before I slipped into the darkness
        inside her
and began my months-long sleep

        where I drew to myself
every gene of him
        chance would grant me,
clenched in my fists,

        and later, was renowned
for carrying home
        wounded birds,
blood-bright leaves, snow, all
things which pass and do not keep.

I Want Now to Bear

I want now to bear the weight
of the name you would have given me,
Father who did not name me,
                              Father
whose palms, at my naming,
lay open and bare
                    and nameless.

I wish to bear the name
birds toss among branches
                of the pines,
names they discard like seeds
before finding the one that gleams
                        in first light.

I want the name you breathed
and shone on the cloth of your robe
            any Sunday morning,
a name that says *grace, fierce,*
                    one spared of embroidery,
a name pierced with what
measure of love you kept
            hidden until your death.

I want now to carry myself beneath
the name you would pull
                from your wallet, folded
and folded over years, the sound I might hear
        as the moon whispering, or the rain
grieving all night
                and into the morning.

At Night for Long Hours I Hear Songs

but it's only the heart
wandering from room to room
        humming to herself, in love
with the chandeliered halls
            of night and day,

and it's the heart who stands at the window
        playing her favourite game:
counting fleecy angels that float along the sky,
        and feeling the exquisite pain
in the way their stray feathers fall
                to earth,
the way everything changes.

And what are stars? I ask her.
        Blossoms in the tree of night, she answers.

And what is dawn?
        Red earth where the sky
            plants its roots.

Call out the companions of childhood,
commands the heart,
            let each bear witness:

the one who died each night
at the hands of her father;
                the one
who kept all the family secrets
locked inside her;
        the one who made a home
high in the arms of the oak
and waited,
        as day gave birth to night,

for the man whose shoes
vanished down the street
  the morning of her conception,
the bright bird of her heart
fluttering in her chest,
  darkness, and no one
inside the lit windows of the house
    noticing her gone.

By the time they came calling under stars,
  already she had grown wings.
  Already she had learned to fly,
     to rise
above the grief-stricken world
   and sing all night.

Something about the Truth

That was the year
        you stopped talking.
Your sister had her friends circle you,
your teacher sent you into the corner.
But you'd stitched your tongue
to the roof of your mouth,
        taped your lips shut,
words a currency you'd forsaken.

Something about the truth
        tapping at your window.
Something about the pieces of your life
that didn't fit.

How little you lived on,
        such crumbs as dreams
of the man who fathered you
wavering at the edge of sleep,
his language *mirage*, his boat's sail
billowing on the horizon
just as light opened your eyes.

Your father's house sleeps
        beneath the moon,
and it is the moon who peers in
where a daughter writes in pen
        on a page;

it is the moon who washes
        his house in light,
unrolls the fabric of its shadow
across the lawn, and the moon
who skims your forehead in sleep.

He's passed your birthday each year
and the date of your baptism
where he pressed his dripping hand
              to your head,
and if you've passed the anniversary
of his death, no one is saying —
              not the birds
who fly over both your houses,

not the wind who enters by the back door
and lifts the pages
              from the piano,
changes the notes and alters the ending,

then leaves by the front door,
ink fading in the address book
              stuffed in his back pocket,
blowing all my candles out.

Father in Heaven

My father in heaven, what do you see,
who are alive to me in your death?
When I look now at the world,
                    I look at it for you.
As if I could name each thing, to remind you.

Every morning I walk the path to the field
where the old horse, woolly
                    from the gathering dark,
meets me at the gate, the sky shining fresh
between the tips of the pines.
Sky, I say. *Horse. The scent of earth.*

The new horse, the wild one, is learning
what it means to live
                    in a field finite and fenced.
He whinnies with the others, allows my hand
stroking his neck,
                    and I say, *touch*,

and think how this light,
                    its waxing and waning,
must seem strange to you now, everything
turning to bronze,
                    a dozen moons
of the horses' hooves pressed into the dirt,

and I wonder whether you think of me
where you are,
                    or if you have found me here
in the field among the horses, and if
I please you with my life.

I Open the Book of Names

I open the book of names
and my index finger calls forth
the procession of ancestors, those
    who have gone before:

a minister-father I never knew;
a mother who searched a profusion
of bedrooms for love that shied away,
        unrequited;

three generations of stones
who slept, every last one, in the quiet sun —
shiftless, the lot of them,
but shone white as pearls
    beneath the moon;

some distant cousins — songbirds —
who once starred on a high wire,
        then flew.
Never called or wrote;

seeds that fell like soldiers in the field
and died before I could know
    if the blossoms of my hands
were descended from any of them;

the wind, who'd stop in now and again,
and was always waving good-bye.

The moon ties back her hair,
              and pensive, turns away,
refuses when I ask for a story.
Though I watch from my pillow,
she will not show her face.

Darkness walks through my house
and visits every room. His hand
strokes my hair until I sleep.

I am daughter to darkness,
              the orphan moon,
while God, wanted for crimes
he didn't commit,
seeks asylum among the stars.

Solstice

each bright glimpse of beauty striking like a bell,
so that the whole world may toll.

— P.K. Page

This winter is all silvered moon and stars, small birds
printing runes into snow, hieroglyph of horses' hooves
frozen in the mud, rimmed in crystalled petals of ice.
Ancient, this world, these fields gone white — a cumulous sky,
each bright glimpse of beauty striking like a bell,

so we may teach ourselves to be whole, and holy
as moonlit lamps of Queen Anne's lace,
so that a whiteness deeper than any of us can know
may shroud the earth to be reborn, and in us a green-belled
    wonder,
so that the whole world may toll.

And in What Darkness

In the longest nights of childhood
I shaped my fleshy hands into wings,
thumbs together, locked
        in a small embrace.

Thus I sent my heart into the night
toward the blinking, bewildered stars.

Thus I sent my heart on the wind
to the moon I claimed as my mother,
her bright skirts flaring, waning.
        My lonely, shining mother.

Oh, the stories she told
of things she'd seen — the wantonness,
        the out and out lies.
What vanished and in what darkness.

Once when I could not find her,
I flew into the white light of heaven.

I didn't know it would be like this, I said.
Promises broken, those who turn,
        those who walk away.
And they placed their resplendent hands on me,

spun me by the shoulders and sent me back.
Grief was not finished with me yet.

And what did I learn Sunday mornings
but even the light, once whole,
                    could break into pieces.
A father commanded to kill his son.
A daughter should be grateful to be a daughter.
              He would only walk away,
having his reasons, his own starry silence.

                    In her sadness
my brilliant mother sewed a moon dress for me,
stitched with thread from the indigo night.
I wore it night and day, my dress,
                    my darkness,
and carried his blood in my veins — my map
of the world, the roads I would travel
looking for him,
              the wind, too, with its shoes on,
waving, carrying on.

Crossing Over

No luck finding him on earth, I crossed over,
a swollen river, scared as I was
to face St. Peter standing glorious
                    before the gates.
We will not all die
but we will all be changed —

Cyrillic script in the arch. He said
it was not my time. He said
                    it was not written
I should so soon meet him,

but I pulled from my pockets
            my offering — shells, stones
of varied stripes and colours,
bottle caps, feathers, an astonishing
array, and asked, *please*, for a day,

an hour with my father — the secret one,
the real one. Then, to break his silence,
                    opened my palm:
a yellow bird, found dead on my porch.

            He took it up and asked
for my bitterness as well — my weed,
my dried stalk, that which
                    would not lie down.
And I gave that over too, and was let in.

There it is always autumn, the dead
      light as leaves, careless
as grass, shining like grain
fresh gleaned from their lives.
Acrobats, they swung from branches,
         translucent bells,

while trees gave over their leaves
to the jasmine, the rose, a great
raining down,
      wild blossoming
green stippled gold, red as sunset, too —
it is always sunset there.
And, brought to my father,
      I showed him the key
to the box of secrets, where I found
his names: *Vanished on the Wind,*
Night's Rowboat,
Flight from Egypt.

To my one allowed question:
I formed you from my seed;
my work in that regard
      was done.
And was ushered back,

though something in me that was his
shone as gold, and windswept
    as I walked among the wet
    stones, making my way
over the rushing water.

I Place My Faith

In this way we are guided through our lives:
your name, signed by your own hand,
waited all my life on a closet shelf
until I uncovered you, folded
      in the dark, and sleeping.

From the wine of my mother's bitterness I grew,
from the black rose of her love,
the brine of your absence.
      My second misfortune —
a father who dwelt in the murky
depths,
      where you lived among the stones
and leaves and lost pennies.
      A grave, Father,
where you prayed your angelic prayers
and not your daughter,
      not even the moon
could reach you.

      I place my faith in grief.
It is what I know. I pray
that I might find the rose of you
tight-wound as a fist
behind the stained glass
      of my irises.
Now in your death, you must live

with the thorn of my love.
I wait for your letters, years old,
                 to arrive, the news
that you were always tormented by God,
and carried your sins, your kit bag of stones
with you to heaven,
         and would not allow even God
to purify you,

            I, the boulder
of your sin, the one you sanctified
in the name of the Father, Son, and Holy Ghost.
I pluck the moon from the branches of pine
         and swallow its light,
that you might be born in me,
             father who speaks
only by silence, whose secrets I hold
in the quiet petals of my hands.

If I lay my ear close against my fingers,
with the patience of ancients,
       will I hear before morning
a thin singing, the distant bell of your voice?
         Each day a new name
I give you — *Midnight. Longing.*
     Eternal. Broken.
       Shadow. Forgive.

This love from which
       you cannot vanish,
this small fire, terrible and tender,
I breathe into life.

Night Begins

Night begins with my mother's hands
weaving a story, a tale
                              within a tale —
one she slipped inside herself,
another she gave to me.

There was a man with golden hair,
it begins, but that story
                              is locked away,
the threads knotted tight
in my mother's narrow fingers.

He came on a quiet afternoon
when bees ravished the jasmine,
          fragrant and wanting.

Night is the shadow birds leave
on the earth when they fly.
Night is the darkness beneath
          my father's shoes
as they go on leaving and leaving.

Night has no bridges,
                    no rowboat,
no map by which the lost are found.

The clack of her loom
                    sang me to sleep,
my mother weaving my story
beneath the closed mouth of the moon,

a fabric she held in her arms, saying,
          here is your life,
the bright thread of my father unravelled,

a story in which a man walks backward
from the house toward the street,
in which bees rise away
from the heartbreaking perfume
        of the jasmine,
a story in which one father disappears
            and is replaced with another.

Much has found a home in this cloth:
            orphaned mittens, dry blossoms,
parables, psalms — all
            calling to each other —
                    a fingernail paring,
the moon of him who is my father;
every house of my childhood
where my mother's secrets
wandered in the night
            clicking doors shut,
pulling windows taut.

To God the Fatherless, pacing the dark
            streets of the cosmos, I pray.
I tell him I belong to no one.

If he'd but turn
                    his cloud-white head,
he'd see me walking through rooms
the day builds, gleaning its fields
for an alphabet
        the birds have left behind,

the *r* in *remember*, the *i* of *silence*,
a *u* to keep them in, the root
            of *found*,
my father somewhere in the bracken of earth or heaven,
        holding his name
in the folded wings of his hands.

– IV –

Without

To begin to live without possessions
           as my father did
one year ago today; simply,
he rose from bed
        and walked out of his life,
leaving everything behind.

           Left his Bible, left his sermons.
Left his piano, his beloved hymns.
Left his lucky penny. Left the dust
        in his pockets.

He did not discriminate. He left
what I longed for him to take:
photographs of me, curved in his wallet,
        grades 2, 3, 5, and on.
Left the note of confession
he'd rather have folded into one palm
and slipped with him
        through the gates.

Left his footprints, quiet as light
        on the stair.
Left the sunlight through his window.
Left the curtains' rising and falling
like someone alive, and sleeping.

Left his toothbrush. Left his teeth.
        Left his breath;
gave it free to the clear, cold air.

I know I could do it; I could live like this —
lived without a father all my life,
then a mother,
          buried in her mind.
And my children who grew wild,
eating everything in sight —
               caterpillars they were;
I watched them burst from cocoons,
               dry their wings in the sun,
departure on their minds.

There were flowers I picked by the bushel
that wilted and died in my arms,
               and the field
I grieved over every summer, thick
with timothy, with brome, cut, bound,
carried away.

I could be stripped bare as winter trees
naked in their branches
like arms reaching overhead —
               frantic, shipwrecked,
and that blue sky, oh, shameless siren
with her high-arched singing
               and falling toward night
swinging her lanterns —
               who could turn away?
Ask him, ask my father if he could.
So true and lovely, that stepping into nothing.

The Birthday

Here the child at the piano,
                    here her hands
suspended over the keys,
                    there her feet
which do not reach the floor.

Evening after supper is the time
reserved for practice,
                    but she fears such music
will shatter what remains
of the ruin of the day,
                    her mother
risen suddenly from the table,
fled from the room, the cake
imperfect,
                    the presents wrong.

She watched it come, sitting beside
          her father's inattention,
as a sky overcome by cloud
crept across her mother's eyes.

Now the great ear of the house
                    listens and waits.
Such waiting is beyond hope;
the depth of this quiet
          is the fist raised just before
it knocks on the door of despair.

The child has been ordered
                to break the silence
that has fallen on the house
and turned the air to stone,
with only the clocks
                to push evening into night,
holding in their hands the secrets

that enter by the innumerable
                small windows in the screen,
                                the shadow
of one who comes and goes from the house
                                in the immaculate noon,
the man whose unknowing
has made him giant.

Presents scattered.
                The cake slumped.
She must press her fingers to the keys:
sunny Clementi, blossoms' frivolous scent
where, in every room,
                                snow is falling.

And Someone Has Died Today

Little songbird,
colour of autumn's first leaf,
you flew toward the trees, the blue
you were born into
            and trusted all your life.

The window lied.
As my mother lied to me
            to save herself, to save
my father, the wrong man
present at my birth.

The honeyed sun
blinds my eyes, too,
the moon has no address,
and your nest is a vacant house
            the wind claims for its home.
I hold you on my palm,
closer than you would ever let me come.

Go, fly through the window of heaven
to my father, ask him
            my true name,
then sing it to me while I sleep,
before the brief, red eye of dawn
wakens the world
            with its own bright grief.

The Heart of the Matter

I was watching my dead father
walk from the street to the house
        in his deliberate shoes,
Christ's resplendent hand on him,
teaching him for all eternity
      never to cast the first stone,
when the couple inside rushed out
        at my unwavering gaze,
with the dog in tow, for defence.

I wanted to explain everything,
how the house held the room
where my father and mother
      traded one darkness
for another, Jesus' many mansions
sacrificed behind a dull curtain
as clouds raced
        over the house, the yard,
and on to the mountains and the place
where God waits in judgement.

But this was not the whole truth.
     I wrung my hands
        and tried again.
It was autumn, the Albuquerque hills
drenched in travelling shadow
and yellow leaves,
      chama weeds
blooming their hearts out.
A fitting welcome for my father,
the waning sun
     lighting the weeds, the trees,
the rose stone of the mountain.

I wanted to tell the couple
　　　　that I meant no harm

but that in his death, my father keeps walking
　　　　from the street to the house
while the wind enters the trees,
　　　　the long light the stone,
and my mother opens the door for him,
as though to hide him from the footfalls
　　　　　　　　of an advancing army,
and that I had saved another room for him, one
I kept dusted, hoping for the day of his return
　　　　which did not come.

Still, I wanted to say, as the door opened,
as they rushed out and my father
　　　　slipped in,
it is all right to believe
in love, to place one's faith
　　　　in the holy
human body, the alabaster jars
just waiting to be poured.

Yet even this is not the heart of the matter.
I must put it more simply:
　　　　I tell you,
there was a hunger in the house.
I knew it even as I rowed my wooden boat
　　　　across the darkening sky.
A man of God,
　　　　carrying his humanness, his lust
into the world.
A god dressed as a man,
　　　　disguised as a gardener.
As our Lord walks, unrecognized, among us.
　　　　My inconsequential voice
mixed with the roar of the milky
river broke open my carapace of sorrow.

From then on
            all I felt was loss.
When the gardener left the house,
already he'd planted me inside her.

Birds watching from a wire
            scattered across the sky
as night fell, a dozen dark stars,
a night that would last half a hundred years.

Everything I Know of You I
Learned from Your Obituary

That you played piano, and lustily, you sang.
That you marked your children with your life.

A sudden, breathing father,
you walked around in me at last.
The eloquence of your prayers was noted.
Evenings you called on congregants in their homes,
and like St. Paul, encouraged, exhorted:
They knew they were loved.
Yes. My mother more than most.

But the list of your offspring missed a daughter.
How I wanted to be the keeper of memories, hold
your stories to my chest, steal your silence
and make of it my own dark music.
Fate said no,
you would be a stranger until your death.
Thus it was written at my birth.

Once, in the holy vessels of your hands, you held me
long enough to proclaim me
a child of God,
sprinkle water on my head, and set me adrift.
Your baby Moses, your darkness.

Now I must be baptized by death to find you
in that place where night is as bright as the day,
the breezy and shadowless rooms of heaven
where there are no secrets,
and nothing is hidden.

My Father Come Down from Heaven

My father has come down from heaven
to his church, to dust the pulpit
with the sleeves of his robe,
        and because memory lives on,
it is the year of my birth again,

and he is placing on each windowsill candles,
and branches of pine,
                their earthly fragrance
filling his nostrils, shadows
falling like dark snow across the floor,

                and he is thinking
how he will dip his hand into holy water
and press the orange flag of my hair,
        Judas the betrayer in a purple robe,
and I in his arms before his congregation
                of the faithful.

But perhaps I confuse the details.
                I was so young.
Was it instead the sharp fragrance
of memory, was it my father's hand
that was holy,
        his hair waving orange?
Did the candles burn orange,
was it I who was Judas,
                the branches of pine
sacrificial, the shadows faithful?

Does the purple robe of the night
            now remember,
and was it my mother pressing shadows
rumpled like a sheet?
Was it her husband or her lover
  who left the bed empty?

Memory wove its nest in me:
it was silence curved into a question:
            Where is your father?
It was the dark bell of the night
            chanting, *gone, gone.*
It was my mother's voice:
            none of this happened,
and the tidy houses who asked,
            which story will you choose?

The small father born inside me says,
The night tells your story.
The day carries the past
            in its pockets.

Tonight, my father goes on dusting memory
with the sleeves of his robe.
            He dusts, and dusts.

Epistle

You arrive like a letter
that has wandered itinerant
    all my life, with news
that your death has rendered you
               invisible.
Now we have traded places, you and I.

At night you walk through your church,
composing in the eternal light of your mind
          an epistle
like St. Paul's to the Romans —
yours, to a congregation of one,
in which you list your sins of passion,
          the sin that gave me my life
and made me to be like you,
one foot planted in this world,
          the other in the next.

You arrive like a letter that has meandered
          across countries,
across snows and melting, and clocks
with their mouths wound shut,
and when I open the envelope at last,
I must sweep up the dust
          of my name,
the crumbled ink of your love.

Tell me, Father, what I should know
about you. What lives inside me
          that is yours.

You arrive, invisible since your death,
                    holding your epistle
to the congregation of one,
your life an ancient city I have never seen
but long to see the sky through the ruined
            porticos of your ninety years.

How quiet is the church
        of holy absence — a forest
birds inhabit, carrying straw in their beaks
to build their own upper rooms,
a church where the dew gathers just before dawn,
its ten thousand leaves
                spattered with stars.

Message for a Time Capsule

Perhaps some of you, coming after, will want to know:
I lived in the time when we stopped speaking poetry
and spoke in prose. That was the start.

Believe me: I saw snow so heavy it broke the roof,
I saw cedars shake their white winter fur.
And moss was shorter but greener than grass.

On our hill, water still ran wild. None of us could catch it.
Dandelions. Daisies. Queen Anne's lace. We had them all.
Even blackberry, prized for its fruit.

There were wars and rumours of wars. The misbegotten words
        rushed past.
How many hummingbirds? I didn't think to count.
In rain, water flared from their wings.

And once I set foot on a great glacial sheet,
but mostly kept to common things:
the clearest blue light beneath the snow,

crystals of ice that grew on windowpanes, rabbits, snails
that sailed around the house and back. This is what I knew of
        earth,
and how we were loved, but failed to love enough.

A Cloth the Colour of Earth

Ask where I came from,
and the answer depends
on whom you ask.

The sea claims I'm her daughter,
tells me I grew inside a shell
inside her,
I, her pearl of great price,
the rain her lover
who climbs down the sky
and adorns her nakedness with stars.

The wind says I belong to no one.
*Don't ask whose you are
and remember nothing,* he says,
but he's just afraid to know
who his parents are.

Ask my mother
with her mouth sewn shut.
Ask her where she went begging
for love.
She'll cup her hands
around nothing, or so it appears,
but it's really the ghost of my father.

Ask my father —
he's rowing a boat across
a sea of loss.
He grows
smaller and smaller each day.
Only his shoes remain on land
and cannot stop
walking away.

Ask me how I came into this world
and I'll say I walked,
starting at the gate of heaven.
Thirsty, I drank from the cup
of the sky.
Hungry, I ate the bread
of sadness
which small birds
placed on my tongue.

If anyone asks, I'll say
a tree rocked me to sleep.
I'll say I learned to read
from the book of tears,

learned to pray
              to a God
whose back was turned,
busy praying to his own God
              and so on,

but sent the moon
              to look in on me,
who taught me to be shy,
to set one clock back
              and one forward,

tie memory into a cloth
the colour of earth,
carry it with me
              all my life.

My Father in his Garden, Depicted in the Woodblock Print of the Taishō Dynasty

For the wooden latch of his heart
      that keeps falling open, for the ten thousand thoughts
      that turn on the hinges of his mind,

for the shape of him, stranded in the weathered branches
      of his bones, for the dark rooted laces of his shoes,
      for his fingernails lined with dirt
      arched as bridges over the stream,

for his shovels and rakes, for the mudded leather
      of his gloves, for leaves
      floating on the pond, and bare trees on sky,

for the creaking ship of him, the mainsail of his shirt,
      his silvered hair wind-tossed,
      his frame tied still to its moorings
      this side of darkness,

for the charting of the seasons, compass of immeasurable stars,
      the rising and falling of light as of the tide,
      and the itinerant clouds mirrored in his eyes,

for the harvest, abundance of petals falling as rain,
      for rain on stone, for small
      belled flowers rung by the wind,

for his sparrows, common as moss, for the feeders
      he fills at dawn,
      for the casting forth, the drawing back of heaven
      at the gate of his heart,

for webs spun and broken, caught
      on the embroidery of air, whose delicacy of lace
      he guards, he keeps watch,

for rain on the still waters of his pond, the darting fish,
      sun's absence and its breaking forth
      as one suddenly emboldened to praise the world

for the small silver music of his voice,
      the name of the unnameable etched in his face,
      for the pondering silence of moon
      hanging over the holiness of his sleep,
      for the twin divinities of his nostrils,
      the centuries of day and of night,

for letters written and unwritten from the brief sacred
      season, the singular blossom of a man's life,

for the signature in a corner of the composition,
      the quiet characters of a name.

The News from Here

Everything went on as usual
the day of your dying.
        A yellow blossom
fell from the winter-blooming
jasmine, foretelling the death
        of winter.

The fly in the window
kept on washing its face,
    a small bird chased a hawk
across the sky,
        and hummingbirds
went about weaving their nests
with twigs impossibly small
wound with the threads of loss.

I walked into and out of the day
not yet knowing you were my father.
        The day you died,
bees came knocking on the window
looking for a way in.
        Whatever they wished to tell me
        was lost, their language
one I once might have spoken,
but have since forgotten.

– V –

One Year to the Day

So light you were
I could have carried you,
as winter's cast-off leaves,
        as a flock of birds,

and crossed the water with you
                in my arms,
though death had made you giant,
the stars dimming, the morning
        rising fragile as breath.

I could have carried you still
        dressed in your plaid shirt
the one you wore the morning
you sank sudden into your chair, overcome
by something like a kiss.
        I could have carried you
alone, I who was bitten thin by absence,
and would have pleaded with him
who held the ring of keys:
                couldn't I, too,
pass through the gates —
I'd polish the furniture of heaven,
        scrub the burial clothes,
hang them to dry in the wind
like ghosts on swings
pumping higher and higher.

So light you were
I could have carried you, singing,
    I your shadow, your shame,
and would have wrapped you
in cloth the colours of dawn
so that you arrived gleaming,
as though you had only
            just been born.

The Sensible Thing

This morning my father, dead a year,
closes the door of his house
and walks the quiet streets
                to his church.

As he breathed his final breath,
his children leaning close,
my father rose from his body
                and walked home.
It was the sensible thing,
the work never-ending, his parishioners
              bent low with their troubles.

So he sets out, hands limp at his sides
and curled slightly,
            like the feet of birds in flight.

          And every morning the wind
blows my mother's dress, green
into his mind,
             and the quietness
with which she stepped out of her shoes.
It was this way when Rome was burning,
and was not so different
            when dark fires flared
outside the walls of Eden.

As my father waits for the walk light,
two clouds dally like children
                    who will not come in from play,
and the cougar just out from his burrow
                    on the mountain,
searches for mice with the bright
coins of his eyes —
                    small loaves of bread
he will hold in his mouth,

praising the holy morning
as my father is doing, the old hymns
          scurrying past in his mind.

In One Country

For a year, my father stood
                beside me in his death,
beating my shoulder with his fist
like ripened fruit falling to earth,
            or the pounding rhythm of rain.

Day and night he stayed, no longer
                    afraid to die,
until the season turned toward darkness,
the soul's bell calling and calling,
            the moon taken hostage.
And my father turned away,
left for another country
where he travelled without luggage,
                    without shoes.

Now I'm back to counting my losses.
Luck crumbles in my hands;
                only echoes resound
from the furthest reaches of childhood.

Let me be the dust in his hair,
                let me be carried,
            a stone in his pocket
as he wanders across death's outback,
the great golden fields bowing,
wave after wave, before him.

My father lives in one country
                    and I in another.
And he who stood at my shoulder
has turned away. Father,
have I disappointed you,
or is it time I knelt inside myself
            and sang my own *alleluia*?

By candlelight I trace the map of my palm
for the road he is walking,
further and further into the vast
                    interior of heaven,
and feel him grow smaller

against the sun that never quite goes down,
the endless steppes
            stretched out before him,
my own night's stars beneath his feet.

Tell Them

Tell the spirits not to come here anymore.
Tell the dead who skim the sky
                    unfettered as birds,
who leave their scarves, their handkerchiefs
snagged in the brittle branches of trees
                    to stop slippering through my door,
            prodigals on the evening breeze.
Tell them I'm tired of living in two worlds.

Make them stop their whispering,
            disturbing my sleep. This dreaming
their faces, their heartrending beauty —
it's no wonder I wake in tears.

When they come famished, wings trembling,
hanging upside down at the feeder,
                    I can't help feeding them,
wanting only to ease their suffering.
And owls — those pale wraiths crying in the night,
feathers of such lustre
            as must be other than of this world,
to say nothing of their eyes.

Or the hundred open mouths, urgent with advice,
reflected in night's window.
            My name isn't my name, I know,
these hands but a resemblance
                    of the one I never knew.
Still, they say, *Choose.*

I have chosen. Let them leave me now.

Just to live on this earth, by the diffident
hands of the clock.
                    Sunrise and sunset. It is enough.
Music unmoored, sails unfurled — a simple voyage
        from west to east, beginning to end,
and the birds only birds, singing
                to waken an ordinary morning
as they gather on the ground,
        gleaning fallen fruit for the seeds of stars.

The Place of Feathers

We saw immediately that they had come,
though they did not come for us.
Out of the great floating cities of the clouds
    they descended
        while we occupied ourselves
with earthly concerns. All around us
the ground laid with a raiment
of feathers —
    oh, what a heavenly multitude
they must have been —
so purely white upon the ground.

I knew they would not come for me.
    Too much I have left undone.
Yet the place could suit for heaven,
    between the underworld of marsh
where cattails root, the hidden portals
where shorebirds sleep,
        and misted fields
green with wheat, stippled stands of willow and oak
    softened in summer's light.

We fell quiet, knowing
    nothing after this would be the same,
the children flying and flown, and we
where we started, believing
    we could understand what love is.

And then dominions of martins in purple robes
rose from the wires,
                    silver underwings flaring —
the thousand minute lamps rising and diving over us,

and a choir of foxes, out from their hollow
                              in the early dark,
yipping, yipping and singing,
praising the bright, the unkempt world.

Winter

The poem: Sparrows lining the sky.

Ice-glazed grass on barbed wire.
From a fencepost, a cat leaps.
The space between branches
where moon and owl wait.

Loneliness: Coyote's eyes on an empty road.

Wind climbing a hill bereft of snow.
Folded over a branch like a discarded shirt,
that leaf, worn thin.
A ship of cloud sailing toward the stars.

Your death: a gate rusted from rain.

An envelope addressed, unsent.
Sleeping under earth, flowers' hard tears.
A boulder above waterline,
the heron flown.

Simple Truths

I wrote a letter to February
                asking how it felt
to carry my father's body, weightless
as a withered leaf, into the earth.
              I explained, too,
how the years had held him in their fists
so that I could not find him
                  while he was alive
with his breath rising into the night air,
his soul only practising
              leaving the body,
the age spots on his hands
a system of planets in their orbits,
my father a galaxy of unknowing,
swirling in the darkest reaches
of my heart.

February said
certain losses, like these, are final.
          No grasping at his robes.
            No chasing after him.
I trespassed the crystal air anyway,
searching for some lost message
etched in stone or on the bronzed
            needles of pines
final and fallen beneath the tree.

I wanted to read his sacred verses,
things he thought a daughter should know:
that the rose blooms
                    because it needs to,
that this earth is nearly heaven,
the rain dripping from the leaves
            each a world like this one,

but in the end could decipher only
      we are given [   ] is enough

February turning its back,
                    humping out of sight
toward a month my father would not
breathe in,
                    the insouciant wind
tossing a dozen winged seeds
sudden into the arms of the sky,
                            in a light like no other,
the last, flared light of day.

The Moon in Her Window

With the moon in her window
        the child opens a book
and begins to read.
In this story, the rose withers
            and the thorns remain;
the moon refuses food and drink
and grows thin until, one with darkness,
not even the stars notice her
trying death on, like a bridal dress.

In the end, my father, a rose
        if ever there was one,
traded his Sunday robe for death,
and now he whispers in my ear:
            Pray, you must pray.

I, who know little of prayer,
watch the horses bow their heads
                to grass,
the bees enter cathedrals of heather,
yet I do not understand prayer
or the way a dead man
        can whisper inside my head
to the child who has never died in me,
but goes on being a child,
and from her window watches the moon
        carefully sewing garments
        for the wedding.

Beyond which night lies the country
           where the dead reside
in houses they need no door to enter,
whose clocks bear no numbers
       and whose hands are leaves
       pressed one to the other?

The child sits cross-legged, paging
through a book for the story
in which the moon
         opens like a rose,
and I, her grown self,
begin without understanding,
to form the words: *Our Father...*

I Sing Two Songs

How ancient were my children at birth,
all heft, burden and gift in my arms.
I sang the night's wilted hours
                    and paced the floor,
the silver coins of their passage
        still locked in their fists.

How young was my father, new-born
                    unto death
and the smoke of embers.
And the father I found after searching
half my life — found him alive,
        awakened after sixty years.
I have seen both of them curled up
asleep like children,
        one with coins in his fist,
one whose passage is spent.

What storm swept my children, my fathers
                    onto the shore
of my own soul's longing?
Was it the loneliness of God,
            or their own straying
into the woods at the edge of heaven,
between the gate fallen shut
and the innumerable doors of the night?
        Hours passing into years,
the clocks growing old,
the windows birds flew through
            from one sky to the other.

Even now, for love, I stroke their heads
as they sleep, my aged travellers,
and sing two songs:
                    diastole and systole,
youth and age, joy and sorrow.
One for the visible,
            one for the invisible,

and pull down the curved needle
                            of the moon,
sew the frayed threads of my children's clothes
into a fabric with my fathers' silvered hair
                and the cupped shells
birds let fall from the sky,
and the unwritten pages
                    of the leaves.
A cover I'll sleep beneath, and dream
of combing their hair, setting each part straight,
                a path through the trees
lit white by moonlight.

Mercy

Let me unlock the doors
    to the night's mute houses
where my fathers lie sleeping,
one dead, one living,
    both breathing.

I can feel the earth's curve beneath us,
the fulgent, fragrant jasmine
    procuring the outer walls,
the small tears in night's fabric.

Let the cats curl up at my fathers' feet.
Let the moon make shadows
    outside their windows —
mouse, tree, owl in shallow flight —
    the moon
multiplied in their fingernails,
and I, rejoicing
    for the lost sheep found,
    one dead, one living.

Sometimes we open our eyes in the dark
    and nothing is the same.
We wake on one side of eternity
    or the other.
Let my fathers wake
    each to his own breath
rising like a soul, or a sparrow's
flight across a field, the swoop and dip
its body makes
    swimming in the air.

Let me cover my fathers with quilts,
anoint their heads with holy oil
the way the Magdalene
           anointed Christ —

extravagant, a torrent of devotion,
beyond all reasonable explanation

for one dead, one living,
                tired now
and resting from their long turning
        and turning of the earth.

AFTERWORD

It happens among poets, painters, novelists, composers — sometimes famously, more often quietly: a thing unnamed and perhaps unnameable, both blessing and curse, takes hold of the creator's being and imagination. A poet or novelist may say that a certain work "wrote itself," that she or he had been merely a conduit for the work whose force and energy seemed to originate in a place deeper than her own sphere of knowing. Alan Paton's *Cry, the Beloved Country* was born in such a manner. The American poet Stephen Berg said of his poems in *With Akhmatova at the Black Gates*, "I kept hearing this voice, and I wrote it down." For the writer, the effect of this intensely personal experience is a kind of shattering, through the poem's or novel's insight which reaches beyond her full understanding; then may follow a measure of resolution, a consolation that something has been said which previously escaped the articulative ability of simple words.

This was my experience in writing these poems, begun around the time of my mother's death. With her dying she took the secrets she had held about her life; also lost, presumably, were the answers to questions I held about my own identity and paternity. As a child, as the younger, the quiet one who arrived home first from school, I seemed to be the only one who knew of her affairs with various men; as an adult I continued to dig for clues to my identity. When I began to focus my search on the minister who baptized me in my infancy, a man who, as it turned out, had died only a few months earlier, something that was locked deep inside me burst open, and the poems which make up *Late Moon* came in a rush. I couldn't have stopped them if I'd wanted to. As well, I felt powerless to write about any other subject. Still, the fact of the poems' creation is no proof that I had found my father or that I could know with any certainty the circumstances surrounding my birth, which found description in the poems. They remain poems, first and last, and come from that unknown place which I may never completely comprehend.

Readers of this book will note that some of the poems refer to a living father; these poems are written for and dedicated to the man whom I call my "adoptive father," who listened and offered his thoughts during the time in which I actively searched for clues to my own beginnings, and who continues to impart his own unique wisdom and humour in many other areas. I dedicate this book also to him, for whom I will always hold the deepest gratitude, affection and love.

ABOUT THE AUTHOR

Pamela Porter is the author of six volumes of poetry and four works for children and young adults. Her poems have earned many accolades, including the 2012 *Malahat Review* University of Victoria 50th Anniversary Poetry Prize, the 2012 *FreeFall* Magazine Poetry Award, the 2011 *Prism International* Grand Prize in Poetry, the 2010 *Vallum* Magazine Poem of the Year Award, and the Pat Lowther Award shortlist. Her novel in verse, *The Crazy Man*, won the 2005 Governor General's Award, the Canadian Library Association Book of the Year for Children Award, the TD Canadian Children's Literature Award, and other prizes. Her latest verse novel, *I'll Be Watching*, was a finalist for the Bolen Books Children's Literature Prize, the Geoffrey Bilson Historical Fiction Award for Young People, and a Texas Institute of Letters book award. Pamela lives on Vancouver Island with her family and a menagerie of rescued horses, dogs and cats.